THIS BRIDGE WILL NOT BE GRAY

Library of Congress Cataloging-in-Publication Data available.

ISBN 978-1-4521-6280-5

Manufactured in China.

MIX
Paper from
responsible sources
FSC™ C104723

Original design by Dan McKinley.
Typeset in Elena.

10 9 8 7 6 5 4 3 2 1

Chronicle Books LLC
680 Second Street
San Francisco, California 94107

Chronicle Books—we see things differently.
Become part of our community at www.chroniclekids.com.

THIS BRIDGE WILL NOT BE GRAY

STORY BY
DAVE EGGERS

chronicle books · san francisco

ART BY
TUCKER NICHOLS

In the beginning there was a bridge.

No, before that, there was a bay.
A bay that led to the ocean.
This ocean was the Pacific.

The passageway between the bay and the ocean was called the Golden Gate. On one side of the Golden Gate was the Presidio, a military base at the top of the city of San Francisco. On the other side there were only hills, green and yellow, rising high above the sea. Beyond these hills were a series of small towns along the coast.

The only way to get to these towns was by boat, or by going very far north and coming back down again. It was not easy.

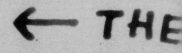

GOLDEN GATE →

So over the years many had proposed building a bridge
between San Francisco and these hills.

But many more thought this a very bad idea.
It will mar the beauty of this land, they said.

What's wrong with boats? they said.

But this book is not about the debate to build the bridge. This book is about the shape and color of the bridge they did build.

In 1928 it was decided to build a bridge, and a man named Joseph Strauss was hired to design it. Originally from Cincinnati, Joseph was an expert in all kinds of bridges.

The first design he came up with was the strangest, most awkward and plain old ugly bridge anyone had ever seen. This is actually what it looked like.

People compared it to an upside-down rat trap. They thought he'd lost his mind.

But he had not lost his mind. He was a scientific man, and he had designed a scientific bridge. It was functional, but it was grotesque.

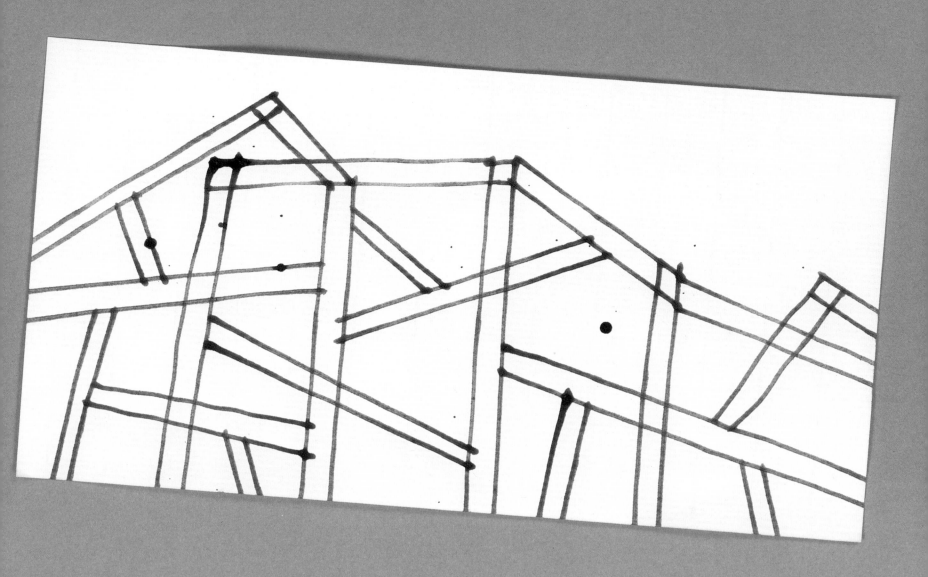

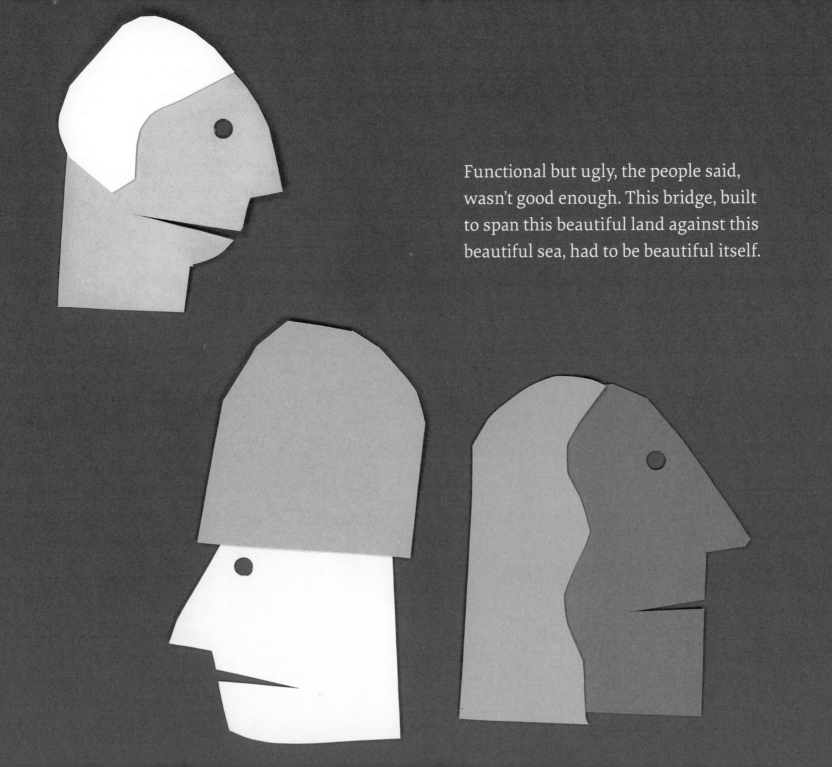

Functional but ugly, the people said, wasn't good enough. This bridge, built to span this beautiful land against this beautiful sea, had to be beautiful itself.

So he tried again.
This time he asked
for help.

One of his helpers
was Leon Moisseiff.
Leon had come to the
USA from Latvia and
had become one of
the most respected
bridge designers in the
world. He designed
the Manhattan Bridge,
which is believed to be
in or near New York City.

Leon designed a suspension bridge,
one with swooping lines and tall towers.
It would be the longest suspension bridge
in the world. It would be the tallest, too.

Everyone was excited
about this design.

I like it very much,
said this man.

My aunt likes it very much,
said this woman.

This third person was chewing food but seemed to agree with the other two people.

But still the bridge appeared a bit stern in style. So Joseph and Leon asked another person, named Irving Morrow, to help out.

Irving Morrow was an architect, and his wife, Gertrude, was an architect, too, and together they lived not far from the Golden Gate. They designed homes, and gardens, but Irving had never designed anything at all like a bridge. Nothing this big or grand or important to so many people all at once.

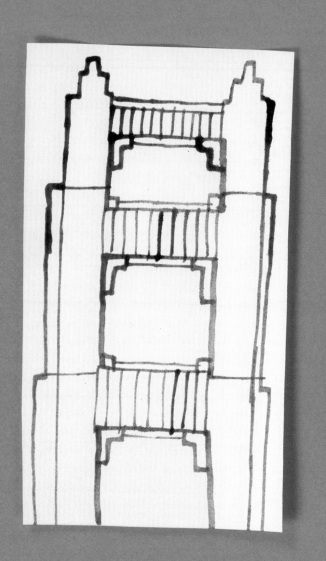
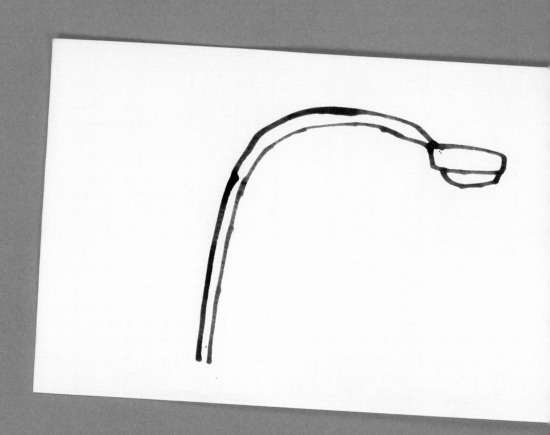

Irving threw himself into the work. He suggested that the bridge have vertical fluting and art deco flourishes. He suggested pedestrian walkways on either side of the bridge. He suggested that there be beautiful lamps along the walkways. Just about none of these things was necessary for the functioning of the bridge—they could have just built it plainer, and cheaper, and quicker—but Irving Morrow thought that the bridge could be both a bridge and something like art. This was a new idea to many of the people who were involved in this project.

So eventually the bridge was designed, and steelworkers in Maryland, Pennsylvania, and New Jersey began building the bridge, piece by piece, in thousands of sections. These sections were put on railcars, and then on boats, and these boats took these parts all the way down the coast of North America, through the Panama Canal, and up the coast of Mexico and California.

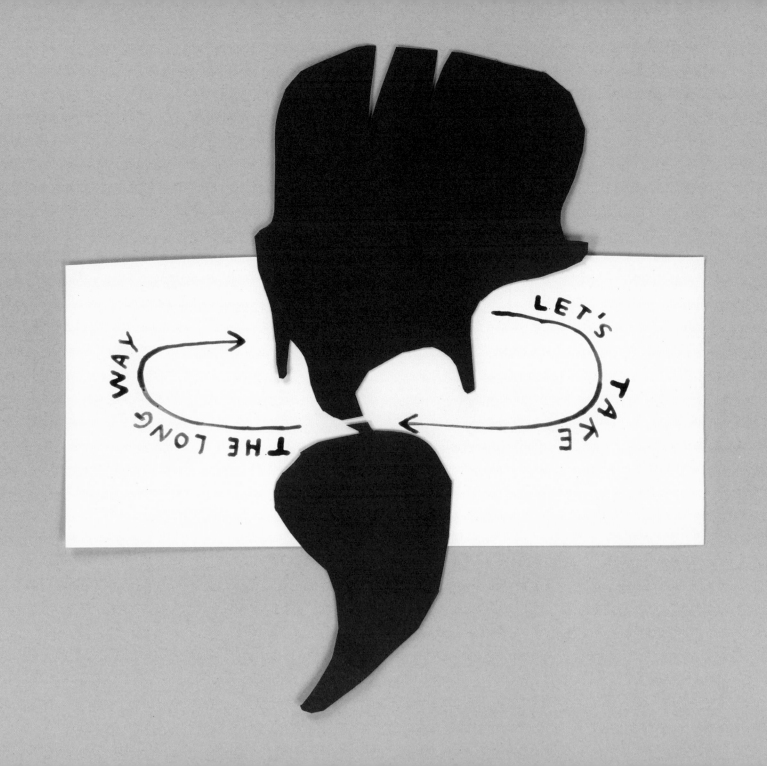

It was a long trip, but the pieces of steel did not mind, for they are inanimate objects.

Finally it was time to construct the bridge. Men had to dive into the freezing ocean to sink the bridge's foundation. Other men, sitting high above the ocean, connected the parts. It was dangerous and complicated work.

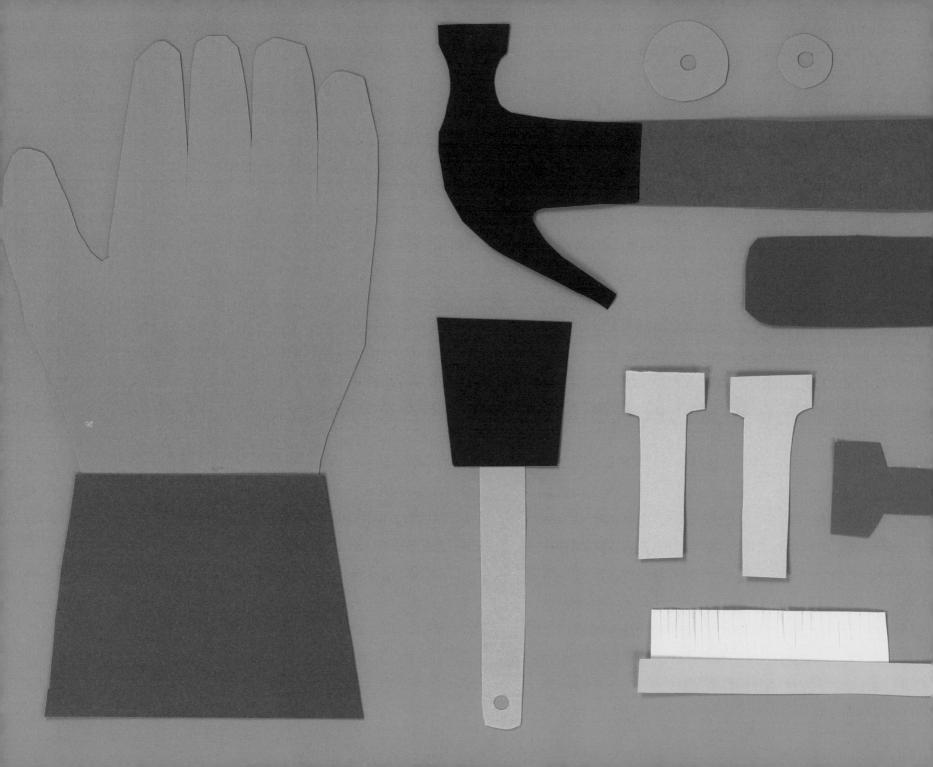

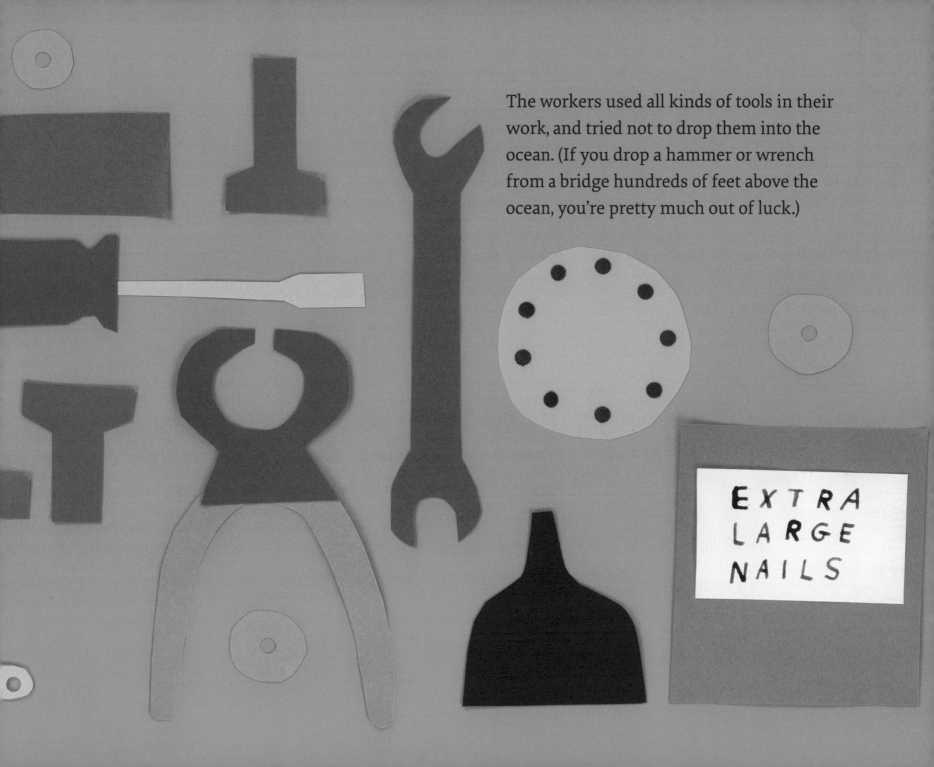

The workers used all kinds of tools in their work, and tried not to drop them into the ocean. (If you drop a hammer or wrench from a bridge hundreds of feet above the ocean, you're pretty much out of luck.)

EXTRA
LARGE
NAILS

Seeing the bridge rise was very exciting to the people of San Francisco and the Bay Area.

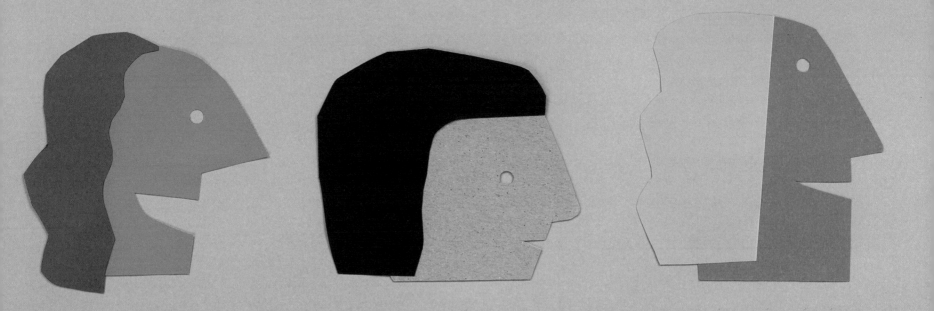

We should stop here and mention that today, San Francisco is a city of about 800,000. It is one of the more unusual cities in the world, given that it's built on and around 49 hills, some of them as high as 928 feet. Have you been to San Francisco? Some of these things you have to see to believe. It is a strange place.

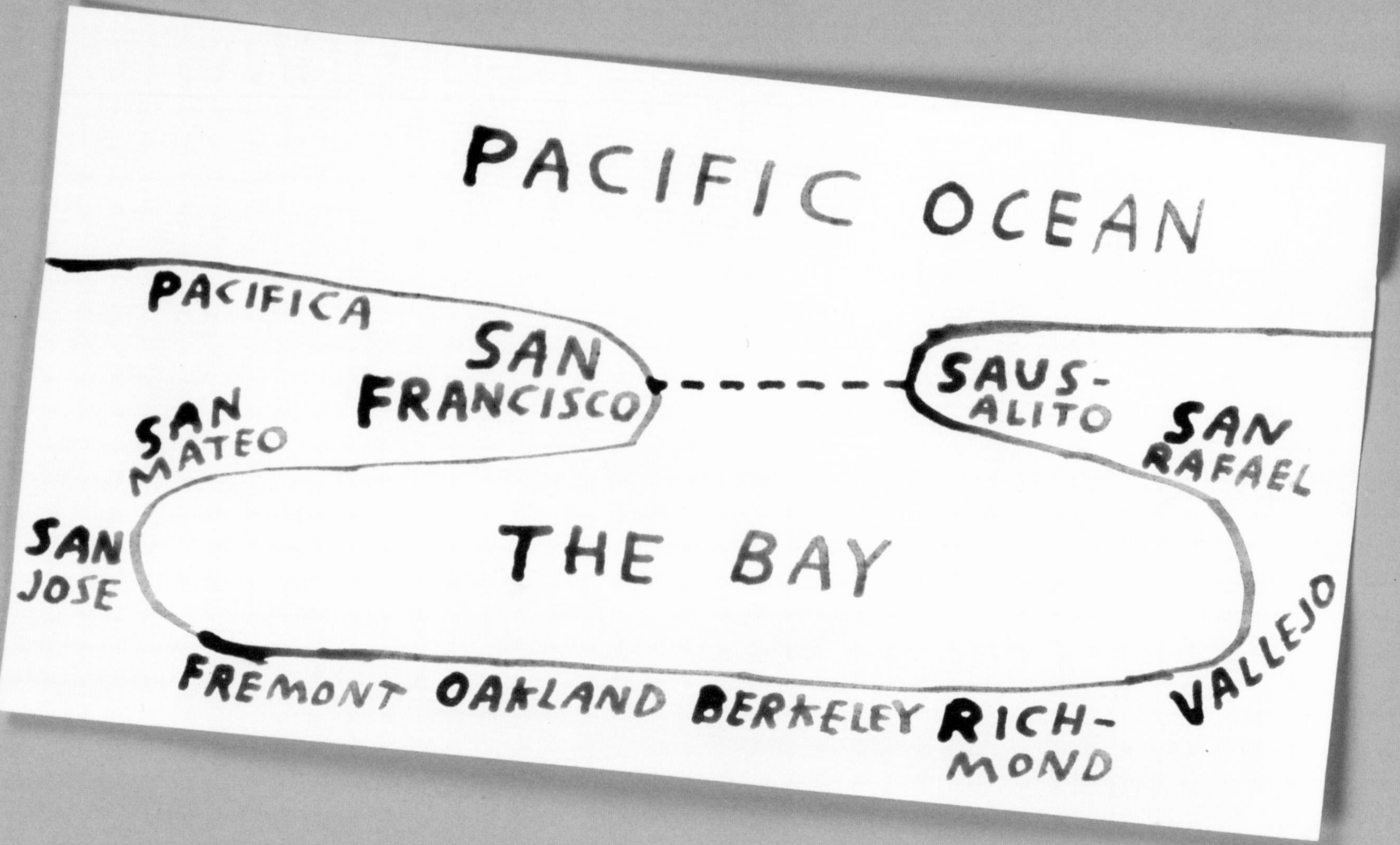
PACIFIC OCEAN
PACIFICA
SAN FRANCISCO
SAUS-ALITO
SAN MATEO
SAN RAFAEL
SAN JOSE
THE BAY
VALLEJO
FREMONT
OAKLAND
BERKELEY
RICH-MOND

San Francisco is one of many dozens of cities and towns built around the Bay. Together, these cities and towns make up a region known as the Bay Area. The Bay it's named for is the one that leads to the Pacific Ocean.

And this bay leads to the Pacific Ocean through the Golden Gate. Remember that? And the Golden Gate was where they were building this bridge.

And it was going up just fine. They estimated
that it would take four years to build it, with
thousands of workers working on it.

But there was one thing that had not been
decided. They had not decided what color to make
the bridge. Isn't that a strange thing, that a very
large group of adults would undertake a project
of this size, and not have a color picked out?

But that's how it sometimes is. In this case,
everyone decided that by the time the bridge
was finished, they would have the color part
figured out.

So they kept building it.

First there were the cables.

No. Wait. First there were the towers.

Of course the towers were first. And they were
astonishing to all.

When the towers were finished, it was a day
of great jubilation. This thing that had not
been there before was now there. The tops of
the towers were 746 feet above the water level.
Sometimes the things humans make baffle
even the humans who make them.

While the bridge was being finished, though, people were still debating the color. And the debate over the color brought forth some very interesting ideas.

The Navy thought it
should be yellow and
black. No kidding. They
did. The Navy thought the
bridge would be safer that
way, so ships and planes
could easily see it.

The Army had a stranger idea: How about red
and white stripes? they said. This is true.
This is a factual book.

The Army wanted it to look like a candy cane for
the same reason the Navy wanted it to look like
a tiger with jaundice: so that it would be easily
seen by planes and ships.

But most people thought these were
not such great ideas. Most people
thought the sensible choice would
be one of the following:

BLACK

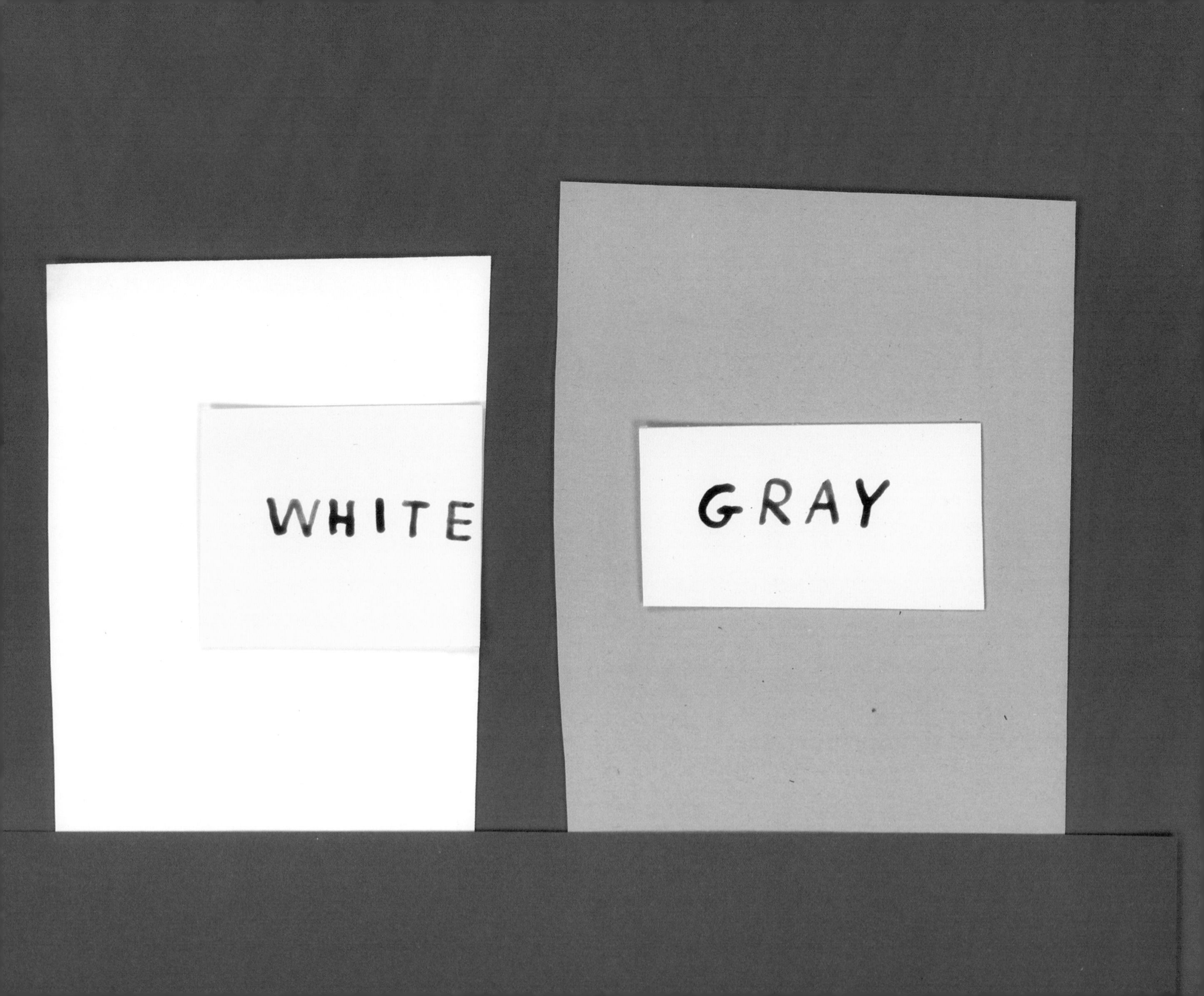
WHITE
GRAY

These were the colors of most large human-made things. Most buildings were gray or black. Monuments and towers were usually white. And almost all bridges were gray. Gray was a serious color. Gray was practical. Gray was dignified. Who could object to gray?

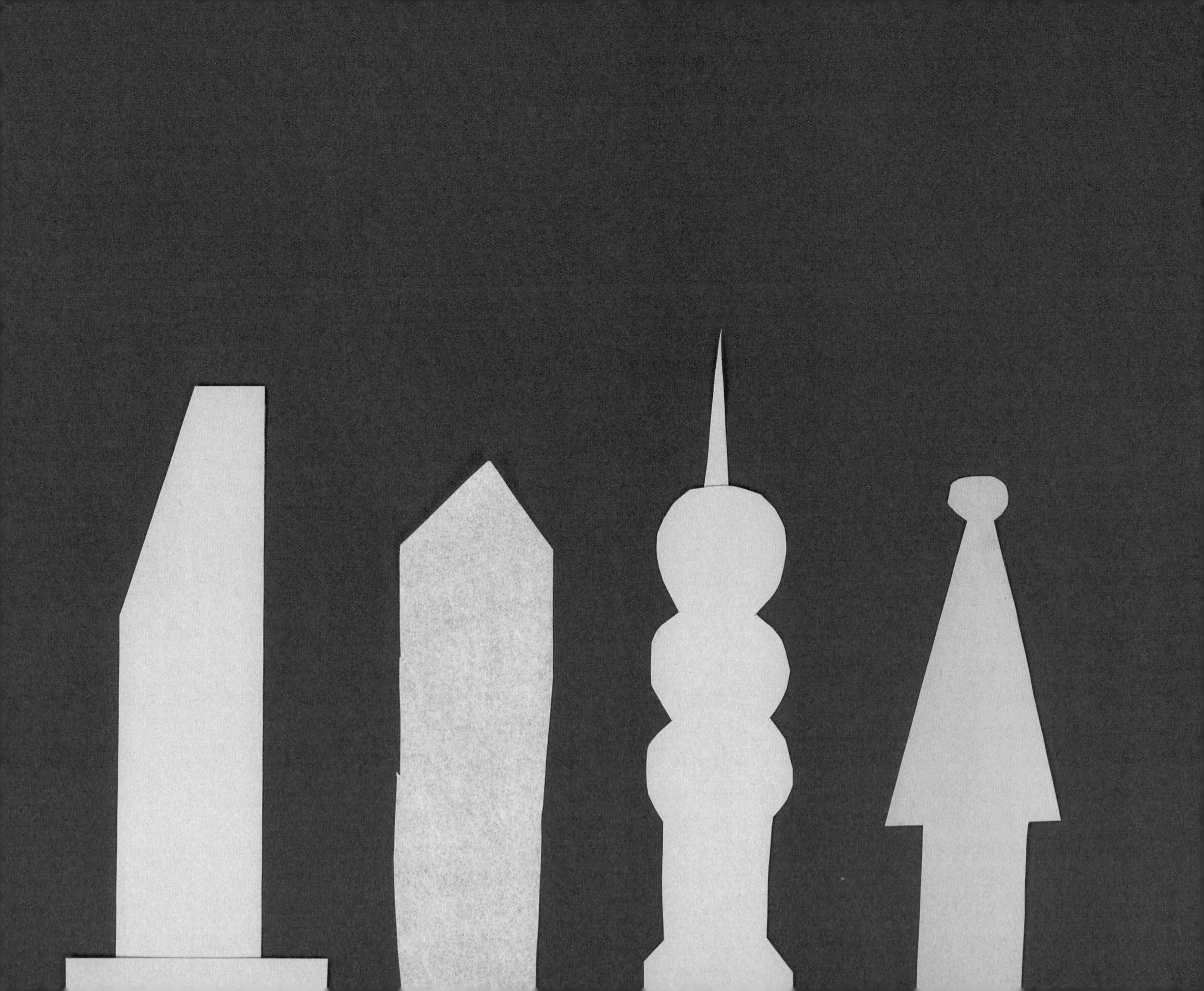

A person named Irving could. And he did.

Irving Morrow had been watching the bridge rise.
He often rode on a ferry out near the bridge, and he
loved seeing the towers rise high above the water.
At that time, of course, the towers were orange.

The steelworkers who had created the bridge in its many pieces had done something before they sent the pieces of the bridge onto the railcars, then the boats, down the coast and through the canal and up the other coast: they had coated the pieces of steel in a kind of paint that prevented them from rusting.

They used this paint all the time. In fact, most of the steel they made and delivered came coated in this same paint. The color of this paint was a certain reddish orange.

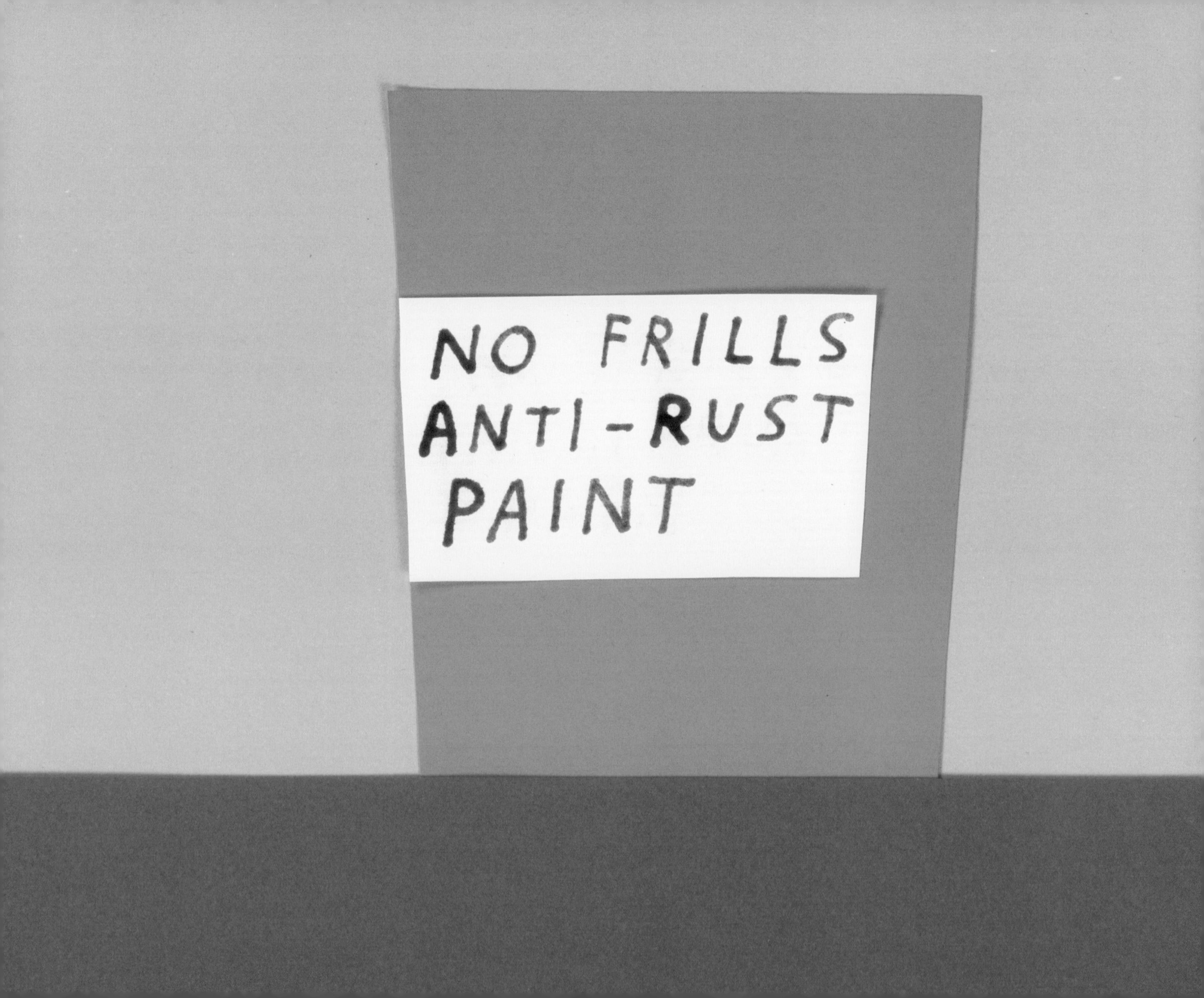
NO FRILLS
ANTI-RUST
PAINT

When Irving Morrow was on the ferry one day, he watched this orange steel being assembled, and he had a thought. He thought that this color was beautiful.

And when Irving was asked what color he thought the bridge should be, he said, Why not leave it this color? And people said, What? And they said, Huh? And they said, Irving, you are nuts. No bridge had ever been orange. Who had ever heard of an orange bridge? No one had, because no bridge had ever been this color. This is true: no bridge in known human history had ever been orange.

And for a good portion of the human race, because something has not already been, that is a good reason to fear it coming to be.

But as the debate continued about the color of the bridge, an interesting thing happened. Other people noticed the same thing Irving had noticed: that this accidental orange somehow looked right.

A woman named Ada Clement noticed.

A man named
Beniamino Bufano
noticed.

And as the bridge continued to rise, and
more and more people saw the orange
steel against the green hills, above the blue
water, below the blue-and-white sky, they
said, For some reason, that looks right.

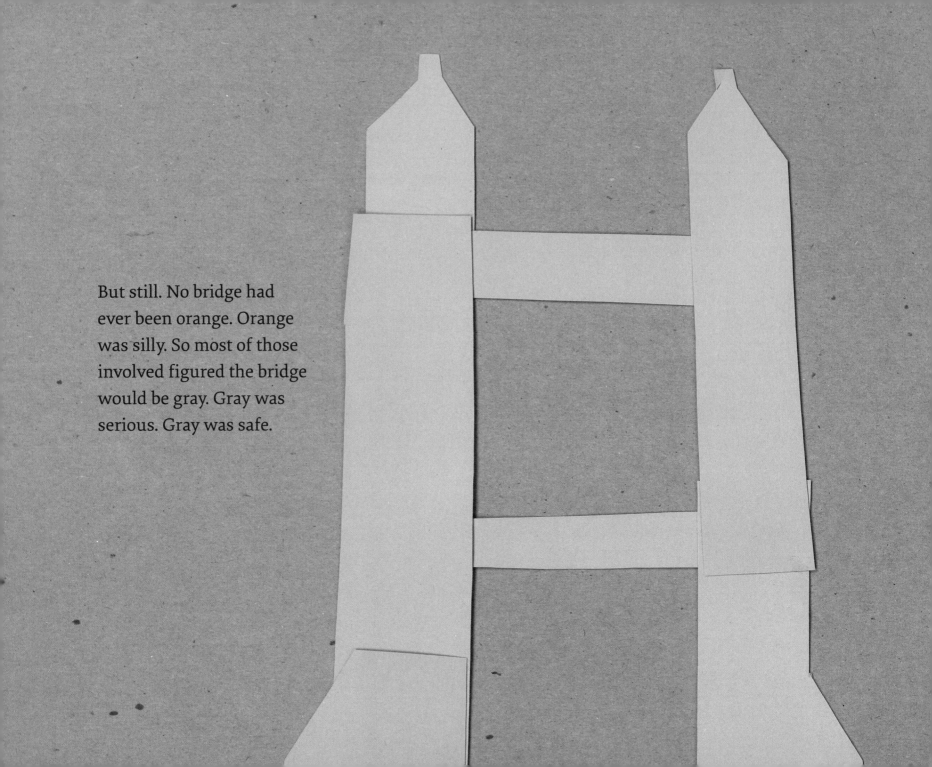

But still. No bridge had
ever been orange. Orange
was silly. So most of those
involved figured the bridge
would be gray. Gray was
serious. Gray was safe.

As they got closer to being finished with
the bridge, though, and closer to painting it
gray, Irving Morrow, who was a quiet man,
who was a shy man, who was no fancy man
with lots of power, began to get loud.

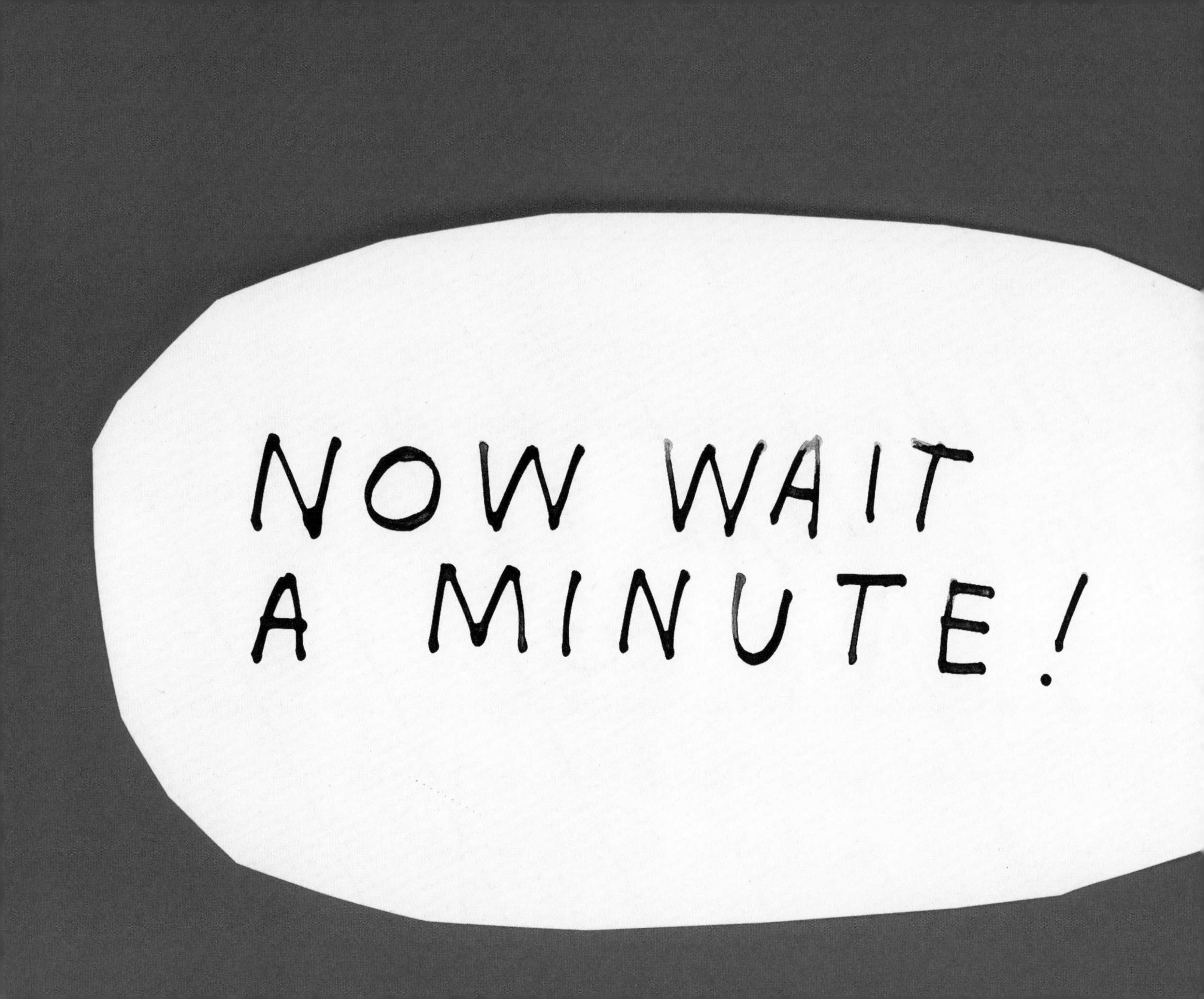
NOW WAIT A MINUTE!

He wrote letters about the orange bridge.
He collected letters from others who believed an
orange bridge was the right thing. And his letters
became louder. And more insistent. He would
have to see this bridge every day for the
rest of his life. He did not want a
gray bridge.

This bridge, he told everyone, will not be gray. This bridge will not be gray.

And others began to echo him.

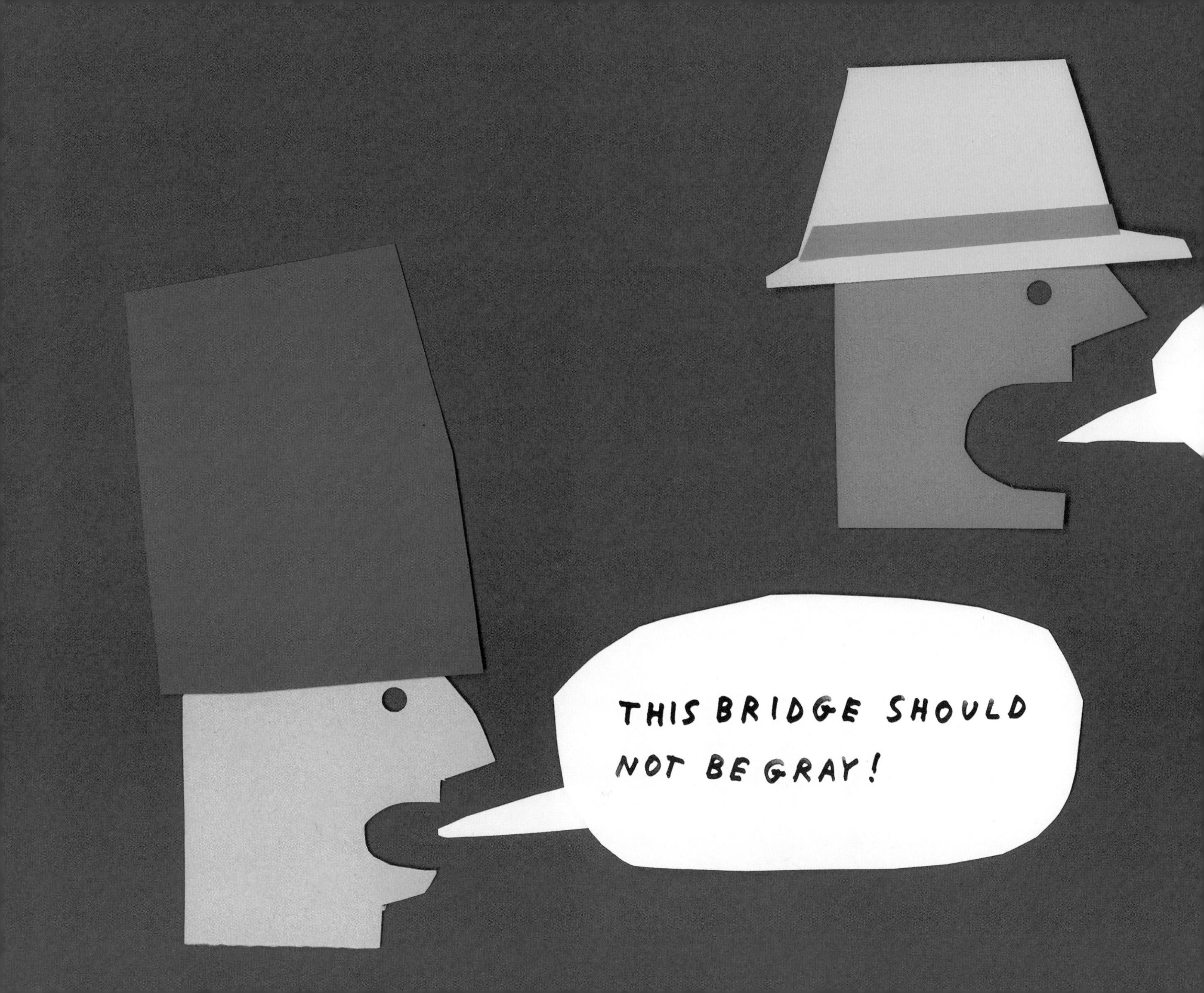
THIS BRIDGE SHOULD NOT BE GRAY!

Finally, the powers that be decided to try it.
And after some time they agreed with Irving that
though it was strange, and unprecedented, and
bold, the orange was the right color.

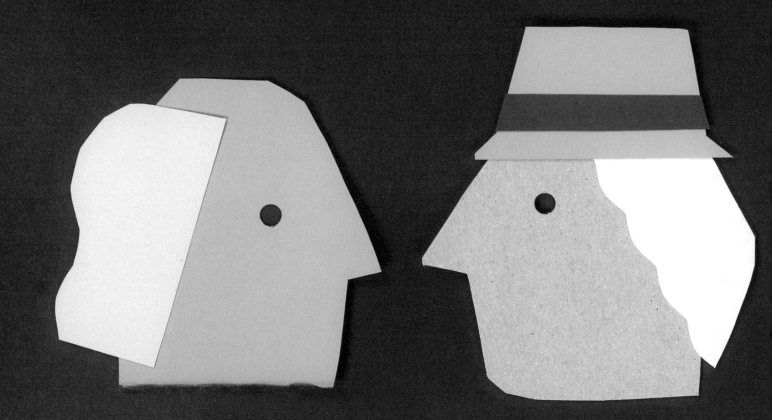

And so it was.

And so it stood.

And still stands today.

You know what they call the color of the bridge?
It has an official name: International Orange.

But because the winds and fog and salt water
in the Bay are harsh, the bridge needs to be
repainted year-round. On any given day,
painters are repainting some part of the bridge.
They use 10,000 gallons of paint a year.

It is crazy that people repaint a bridge all year. It is crazy that people repaint an orange bridge all year with all that paint. But people love to paint it, and people love to look at it. The Golden Gate Bridge, which is orange, is the best-known and best-loved bridge in the world.

It is best-known because it is bold and courageous and unusual and even strange. It is best-loved because it is bold and courageous and unusual and even strange. And it is all these things because Irving Morrow, and thousands of others said:

THIS BRIDGE   WILL

NOT BE GRAY!

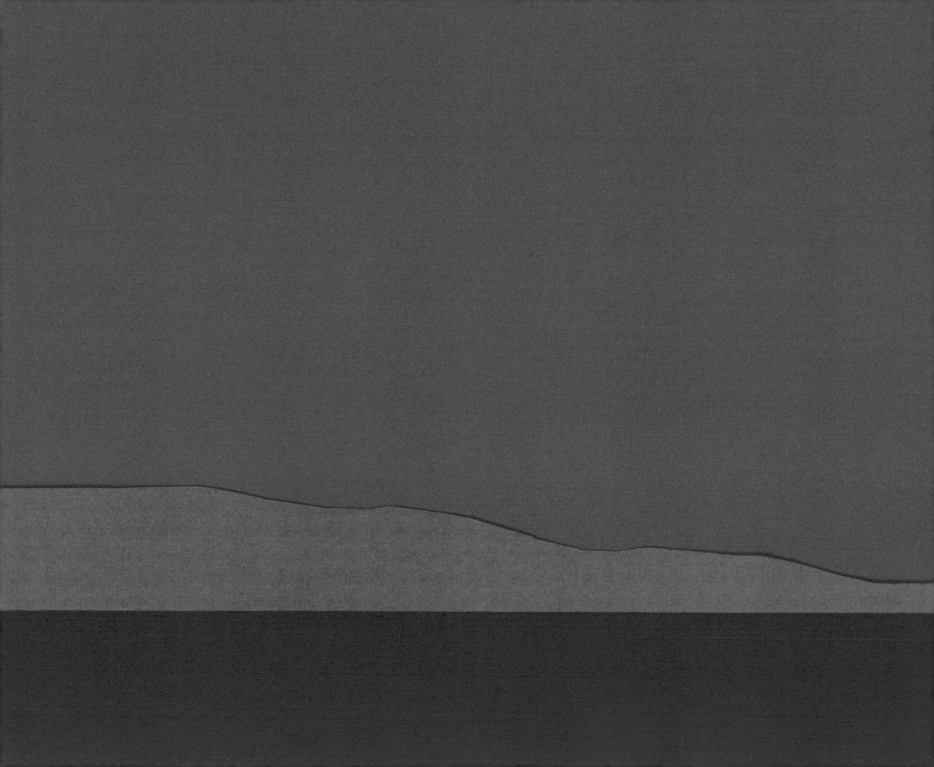

The End

Dear Mr. Morrow -

  I have been watching very closely
the progress of the towers on the Golden Gate
Bridge in its structural beauty its engineering
and architectural simplicity - and of course its
color that moves and molds itself into the great
beauty and contours of the hills - let me hope
that the color will remain the red terra cotta
because it adds to the structural grace and
because it adds to the great beauty and the
colorful symphony of the hills - and it is
because of this structural simplicity that
carries to you my message of admiration in this
note - this comes to you with my warmest thought
and wishes -

  I am

    (signed) Beniamino Bufano

ENCLOSURE A

COPY

SAN FRANCISCO CONSERVATORY OF MUSIC, INC.
3435 Sacramento Street
San Francisco

Telephone Number Walnut 3496

March 2, 1935

Mr. Irving Morrow,
De Young Building,
San Francisco, California

My dear Mr. Morrow:-

  I am writing to you as
architect of the Golden Gate Bridge to
protest against having a black bridge on
our side of the Bay as I see projected
from the Oakland Bridge.

  As a commuter from Mill
Valley it has been a daily joy to me to see
the beautiful red towers against the sky
and Bay and I would like to put in a plea
that that color be made its permanent
color. Our Golden Gate with its marvelous
variety of colors at sunset and sunrise is
one of the joys of all true San Franciscans
and one of the sights which visitors most
comment upon. I believe these beautiful
towers will enhance this if they are light
in color and know that my opinion is shared
by a large number of people who travel
across the Bay.

  Very sincerely yours,

    (signed) Ada Clement

AC:CS

COPY

ENCLOSURE C

MILLS COLLEGE
School of Fine Arts
Art Gallery – Department of Art
MILLS COLLEGE – CALIFORNIA

March 11, 1935.

Mr. Irving F. Morrow
de Young Bldg.
San Francisco, Calif.

Dear Mr. Morrow,

    In answer to your question, what is the best color for the Golden Gate Bridge, I would say this:

    At those times of day when the bridge is to be seen mainly as a silhouette, early morning before the sun strikes it, and late afternoon when the sun is about to set, it would not matter much what the color was. But, since these periods of day are relatively short, it seems to me that the bridge should be painted a color best suited to its appearance between the hours of eight in the morning and five in the afternoon, as well as at night.

    As a point of aesthetics it would be essential that the color of the bridge did not tend to make it melt into the sky. To avoid this, certainly any colors similar to sky colors should not be used, such as gray or even aluminum. It would also be a mistake I feel to use black since then the bridge would be sombre and unfriendly, and most important, it would lose a great deal of beauty of pattern which a warm color would bring out.

    It would seem to me then that a rich warm color would be the best for both day and night, especially since a warm color would make a more beautiful contrast to the cool colors of sky and ocean which form the greatest part of its background. I think this point was rather well illustrated during the P.P.I.E. when Mr. Maybeck had the doors of all pier sheds painted an orange red.

    Very sincerely yours

    (signed) Warren Cheney

    Warren Cheney, Lecturer in Art

ENCLOSURE B

MRS. LESTER L. ROTH
3355 Pacific Avenue
San Francisco

Mr. Irving Morrow,
de Young Building
San Francisco

Dear Sir:

    The other day, I expressed admiration for the lovely color to which the red paint on the Golden Gate Bridge had faded; to Jane Berlandina Howard who in agreement, said you thought so too; and would I write and tell you. Here it is "We want red Bridges".

    How many "seconds" do you need to put your "notion" through? Here are a few.

    Cordially yours

    (signed) Marion R. Roth
               & Lester L. Roth &
               Marion E. Roth
               Annemarie Geller

Saturday

ENCLOSURE H